SIXTY-MINUTE SEDER

PRESERVING THE ESSENCE
OF THE PASSOVER HAGGADAH

by Cass (Yickezkale) & Nellie (Nechama) Foster
Foreword by Rabbi Judith HaLevy

SIXTY-MINUTE SEDER

PRESERVING THE ESSENCE OF THE PASSOVER HAGGADAH

A Simple Guide to a Traditional Seder
Including Easy Recipes

by Cass (Yickezkale) & Nellie (Nechama) Foster

Foreword by Rabbi Judith HaLevy

A division of Five Star Publications, Inc.
Chandler, Arizona

Linda F. Radke, President
Five Star Publications, Inc.
PO Box 6698
Chandler, AZ 85246–6698
480–940–8182

www.FiveStarPublications.com
www.SixtyMinuteSeder.com

Publisher's Cataloging-In-Publication Data

Foster, Cass, 1948-
  Sixty-minute Seder : preserving the essence of the Passover Haggadah
: a simple guide to a traditional Seder including easy recipes / by Cass
(Yickezkale) Foster & Nellie (Nechama) Foster ; foreword by Judith HaLevy.

    p. : ill. ; cm.

  Issued also as an ebook.
  ISBN: 978-1-58985-260-0

  1. Seder. 2. Haggadah. 3. Passover cooking. I. Foster, Nellie. II. HaLevy,
Judith. III. Title.

BM695.P35 F67 2013
296.4/5371   2013934336

Electronic edition provided by

 eStarPublish.com

the eBook Division of Five Star Publications, Inc.

MIX
Paper from responsible sources
FSC
www.fsc.org   FSC® C002589

Printed in the United States of America

Cover Design: Kris Taft Miller
Page Design & Layout: Kris Taft Miller
Editor: Paul M. Howey
Proofreader: Patricia Kot
Project Managers: Patti Crane and Cristy Bertini
Consultant: Netzer Maoz

The Kotel, or The Western Wall, is part of the remains of the 2nd temple, built in 516 B.C.E. and destroyed in 70 C.E. It is the most significant site in the world for most Jews.

- Photo by Cass Foster

Contents

Foreword

The original Passover celebration, described in Exodus, was probably a sixty-minute Seder. "This is how you shall eat it," the fleeing Israelites are told. "Your loins girded, your sandals on your feet, and your staff in your hand; and you shall eat it hurriedly, it is a Passover offering to the Lord." (Exodus 12:11). The Israelites left "*b'chipazon,*" in great haste, and there was hardly time for a five-hour discourse before the paschal lamb was served.

G-d instructs the Israelites and all future generations to be ready to respond when your children ask you, "What do you mean by this rite?" (Ex 12:26). I am certain our fleeing fathers answered those gathered in sentences that were precise and to the point!

L'dor v'dor: We are commanded to retell the Passover story from generation to generation. The challenge is that we have been telling our story for more than 3,200 years, and each year adds a new dimension to the telling. What was perhaps an hour-long tale of rescue and redemption is often a marathon of Jewish storytelling. Are we there yet? For many, the prospect of a complete Seder seems so daunting that the leader gives in to hungry pleas and a flurry of noisy kitchen activity soon after "Dayenu." It is enough. The Seder, an order of ritual and blessings, never really happens. We ran, they chased us, we won. Let's eat.

But there is a Seder, an order that has sustained the Jewish people throughout our long history, destined to be told to our children and their children's children. Cass and Nellie Foster have done an amazing job of sifting the essence of the Passover ritual from the embellishments of time. Each section is explained clearly, with the appropriate blessings in Hebrew and transliteration. The symbols are explained in a manner accessible to Jews and non-Jews alike. The classic songs are included, with some new versions as well. The outstanding glossary of terms makes it possible for a newcomer to understand the background of the symbols and rituals without adding long readings to the text. Pre-Seder preparations are explained clearly. Best of all, Nellie's family recipes make it possible for anyone to create a "Splendid Seder Meal" (see page 58). She even spills the closely guarded "Manischewitz matzah ball and soup mix" secret. Quinoa-stuffed peppers are a perfect match for our "foodie" times, and "coffee matzah" really got my attention!

We live in an age of *chipazon*, where everything happens quickly. We text and tweet (hopefully not at the Seder table) and can describe almost anything in 140 characters. We are commanded to "tell the story to our children," but we must do so in a time frame that will encourage them to hear it. Cass and Nellie Foster's *Sixty-Minute Seder* brings the essence of Passover to the table. Pass it on, and enjoy!

— Rabbi Judith HaLevy
Malibu Jewish Center and Synagogue

Preface

A Seder in an hour? To a traditional rabbi, it sounds like heresy! But you now hold an opportunity to discover a truth about this long-standing ritual that is often obscured by the focus on form over substance.

The order of the Seder is a framework for building your own story of liberation. Cass and Nellie Foster have distilled it to its essence. And I dare you—maybe double dare you—not to be captivated by the opportunities they present.

That's not to say that a sixty-minute Seder is not itself a fulfillment of the expectation that in every generation we see ourselves as having been personally liberated. The number of minutes devoted to reciting blessings or recounting commentaries is not prescribed.

If you follow the instructions in this edition, you will indeed create the next link in an unbroken chain of tradition that begins when "We were slaves to Pharaoh in Egypt."

Rather, the significance of each of the fifteen steps will generate a hunger within you to know more, to do more and to experience more, if not around next year's Seder table, then certainly in the twelve months between this

Seder and the next. Like the wonderful meal you will enjoy, digesting takes longer than consuming. (And sometimes the leftovers are even more delicious!)

Look around the table at the community formed to celebrate. If you number two or twenty or two hundred, the hour (or more) you spend with this Haggadah will create memories and motivations, whether next year in Jerusalem or here again with family and friends.

— Jack Moline is the rabbi of Agudas Achim Congregation in Alexandria, Virginia. He also serves as an adjunct faculty member of the Jewish Theological Seminary and Virginia Theological Seminary and is active in civic and advocacy organizations.

Why Is This Haggadah Different From All Other Haggadahs?

My Orthodox grandparents, David (Z"l) and Emma (Z"l) Weiss, emigrated to the United States from Hungary in 1929 with their nine children. Needless to say, if they remained much longer, I wouldn't be here to create this Haggadah along with Nellie, my beautiful bride of over twenty-five years.

I was born and raised as a Conservative Jew in Northwest Indiana (I won't mention the name of the city because if I do you'll break out in some silly song) and was fortunate to have lived in a very close and tight-knit Jewish community. Between my Mom (Z"l) and Dad's (Z"l) side of the family, I grew up with twenty-eight aunts and uncles and forty-eight first cousins. It was a good life and I sorely miss living in a neighborhood where we knew everyone, watched out for each other, walked to the Shul together, celebrated the high holy days together, and rarely locked our front door. Of course, I also miss purchasing gas for twenty-five cents a gallon.

My grandparents' Seders were long. The two things the grandkids looked forward to the most were hiding the

Afikomen (*if it was our turn*) and playing outside once the meal was over. Otherwise there were a lot of restless folks—and not just kids. Hey, we knew the story and how it ended. And did I mention their Seders were *lonnnng*?

Nellie and I continued the tradition of hosting a first-night Seder and typically accommodated forty-five to fifty guests. In the early '90s I wrote a series of *Sixty-Minute Shakespeare* plays so the standing joke was "How about a sixty-minute Seder?" Over the years I've put many a Seder guest to sleep. As I age, I find I'm even putting myself to sleep. So I figured an hour-long version might not be a bad idea.

Then it occurred to me that others might appreciate a condensed version that covers what needs to be covered and in the prescribed order. (Seder, after all, means order.) And not only Jews: We have numerous Gentile friends and relatives who are invited to and attend Seders. I suspected they'd appreciate a service lasting less than two to five hours that provides everything they need to know, from the planning to the actual enactment of the Seder.

I couldn't tackle this alone, so I'm glad to say it took little effort to convince Nellie to assist me. She agreed that there was a need and loves the idea of helping others plan their Seders. And we both felt the Haggadah should be as comprehensive as possible. So those were the seeds that led to the *Sixty-Minute Seder: Preserving the Essence of the Passover Haggadah*.

When we approached Five Star Publications, Inc., Linda's first question was, "What makes this Haggadah different?" Our response was, "Everything." It's a traditional (though condensed) Seder, honoring and observing Passover by making each step in the entire process clear and accessible.

There are at least 3,500 types of Haggadahs and they specialize in kids, Zionism, feminism, civil rights, vegetarians, Messianic, Ashkenazi, Mormonism, Sephardic, Orthodox, Conservative, Reform, Christian and so many more. Because of the brief discussion period built into this Haggadah, you can focus on anything that interests you or your guests.

For those interested in more gender-neutral prayer books, we encourage you to change any male reference to G-d or our Lord as you read aloud to what makes you comfortable.

Possibly Lord, Sovereign Lord, Lord on High, Holiness, Adonai, Blessed One or whatever description you see fit to describe our most Sovereign Lord. What's important is that you make this Haggadah and this Seder work for you and your family/guests. In spite of all the *tsoris* we live with, this is an incredibly special and joy-filled time. Make this experience your experience.

Ultimately you'll select the Haggadah that helps you and your guests better understand, appreciate, and enjoy the beauty, fun and holiness of the annual Seder experience and we're honored to be invited into your home and included in your Seder.

We'd love to hear from you about how well (or poorly) our Haggadah served you. If critical, we'll cringe but consider for reprints. If positive, it might be used, with your consent, in Five Star's promotional efforts.

Todah Rabah and hoping you have a happy, healthy, and kosher Pesach!

— Cass & Nellie

- Photo by Ian Foster

*To Sarah
bat Meir Avraham*

Candle Lighting

(Page 49 provides additional information)

Two blessings are recited. Either the first and third, or the second and third.

1. Recited once kindled when Passover falls on Shabbat:

Baruch Atah Ado-nai, Elo-heinu Melech Ha-olam, Ah Sher Kee-Deh-Shah-Noo Beh-Mitz-Voh-Tahv Veh-Tzee-Vah-Noo Leh-Had-Leek Ner Shel Shah-Baht Veh-Shel Yohm-Tovh.

Blessed are You, Lord our God, King of the Universe, Who has sanctified us with His commandments, and commanded us to kindle the Shabbat and Yom Tov light.

2. Recited when Passover does not fall on Shabbat:

Baruch Atah Ado-nai, Elo-heinu Melech Ha-olam, Ah Sher Kee-Deh-Shah-Noo Beh-Mitz-Voh-Tahv Veh-Tzee-Vah-Noo Leh-Had-Leek Ner Shel Yohm-Tovh.

Blessed are You, Lord our God, King of the Universe, Who has sanctified us with His commandments, and commanded us to kindle the Yom Tov light.

3. The following blessing is recited after the first or second:

Baruch Atah Ado-nai, Elo-heinu Melech Ha-olam, She-heche-yanu, V'kiye-manu Vehigi-yanu La-z'man Ha-zeh.

בָּרוּךְ אַתָּה אֲדוֹנָי אֱלֹהֵינוּ מֶלֶךְ הָעוֹלָם, שֶׁהֶחֱיָינוּ וְקִיְּימָנוּ וְהִגִּיעָנוּ לַזְמַן הַזֶּה

Blessed are You, Lord our God, King of the Universe, Who has kept us in life, sustained us, and enabled us to reach this season.

The Seder Service Begins

1. Sanctifying the Day: *(With KP wine or KP grape juice)*

Kadesh קַדֵּשׁ

Text in the gray boxes is to be spoken alternately by individual guests. The goblet icons indicate the change in readers. Clearly not a simple request for those consuming four cups of wine. And no whimpering. It is much less painful than your fearful leader doing all the reading. Please note italicized print is rarely spoken aloud. The Leader will announce in Hebrew and English the name of each of the fifteen steps prior to starting each step.

Welcome to our Seder. I'd like to acknowledge those who made significant contributions to help make this very special evening possible. Thank you to_____. Yasher Koach! *(Thank you and may your strength be increased.)*

Whether you're family, friend or acquaintance and regardless of your religious affiliations, we're honored to have you here with us to celebrate this mitzvah. This is a very special evening and your being here makes it even more special. Thank you.

And we thank You, Lord Our God, for the gift of this Passover, the festival of our liberation, a day when we are obligated to recall our Exodus from Egypt nearly 3,500 years ago.

 It's time to fill our first cup of wine but throughout the night, instead of filling our own, we will fill someone else's so we are reminded of how special and how loved we are.

Let us fill our wine *(or grape juice)* cups but not drink yet.

We raise our cups in our right hand and recite the following prayers first in Hebrew and then English:

Baruch Atah Ado-nai Elo-heinu Melech Ha-olam Bo-reh Pree Ha-ga-fen.

בָּרוּךְ אַתָּה אֲדוֹנָי אֱלֹהֵינוּ מֶלֶךְ הָעוֹלָם, בּוֹרֵא פְּרִי הַגָּפֶן.

Blessed are You, Lord our God, King of the Universe, Who creates the fruit of the vine.

Words in parentheses when Passover falls on Shabbat.

4

Blessed are You, Lord our God, King of the Universe, Who has chosen us from all peoples, and has raised us above all tongues, and has sanctified us with His commandments. And Thou hast given us, O Lord our God, in love, (Sabbaths for rest and) Festival of Matzah, the season of our freedom, (in love) a sacred gathering in memory of the departure from Mizrayim. For Thou hast chosen us for our inheritance (Thy Sabbath and) Thy appointed holy times (in love and favor) in rejoicing and gladness. Blessed art Thou, O Lord, Who sanctifies (the Sabbath and) Yisrael and the festivals. *(We say, Amen.)*

If Pesach falls on Saturday night, gaze at the lit candles and recite the following: (If it does not fall on Saturday night please continue with "This blessing is recited..."*)*

Baruch atah, Adonai, Elohaynu melech ha'olam, boray me'oray ha'aysh.

Blessed are You, Lord our God, King of the Universe, Creator of the fire's light.

Blessed are You, Lord our God, King of the Universe, Who distinguishes between sacred and secular, between light and darkness, between Israel and the nations, between the seventh day and six days of activity. You have distinguished between the holiness of the Sabbath and the holiness of the festival, and You have sanctified the seventh day above the six days of activity. You distinguished and sanctified Your nation, Israel, with Your holiness. Blessed are You, Lord our God, King of the universe, Who distinguishes between holy and holy.

This blessing is recited to express gratitude and appreciation when we do or experience something new, or renewed— when we put on new clothes, enter a new house, eat a new fruit for the first time in the season, celebrate a Jewish holiday, fulfill a mitzvah, or see a friend whom we haven't seen for some time.

The Shecheyanu is derived from the word *chai* —meaning life. It's our appreciation for being alive and for the power to use life for worthwhile ends. Let us recite the Shecheyanu in Hebrew then English:

Baruch Atah Ado-nai, Elo-heinu Melech Ha-olam, She-heche-yanu, V'kiye- manu Vehigi-yanu La-z'man Ha-zeh.

בָּרוּךְ אַתָּה אֲדוֹנָי אֱלֹהֵינוּ מֶלֶךְ הָעוֹלָם, שֶׁהֶחֱיָינוּ וְקִיְּימָנוּ וְהִגִּיעָנוּ לַזְּמַן הַזֶּה

Blessed are You, Lord our God, King of the Universe, Who has kept us in life, sustained us, and enabled us to reach this season.

While reclining, we enjoy in our first cup of wine. Please drink only when indicated throughout the Seder.

2. First Ritual Hand-Washing:

Urchatz וּרְחַץ

It's permissible for me to serve as a proxy for all, though you are all certainly welcome to accompany me. Water is poured three times on the right hand, then the same on the left hand. We dry our hands and return to the table.

As the Leader proceeds to wash his/her hands:

Jews are obligated to perform the spiritual cleansing of the washing of their hands before each meal. This is the only time of year we do not recite a prayer while washing our hands. Please be sure to remove any rings.

3. Dipping Parsley in Saltwater:

Karpas כַּרְפַּס

Leader rises and briefly holds up the Karpas.

Let us recite the following in Hebrew, then English:

Baruch Atah Adonay elokenu melech haolam boreh pree ha'adamah.

בָּרוּךְ אַתָּה אֲדונָי אֱלֹהֵינוּ מֶלֶךְ הָעוֹלָם, בּוֹרֵא פְּרִי הָאֲדָמָה.

Blessed are You, Lord our God, King of the Universe, Who creates the fruit of the earth.

All eat parsley or celery dipped in saltwater.

4. Breaking the Middle Matzah:

Yachatz יַחַץ

The Leader holds up the middle matzah.

ALL: This is the bread of affliction that our fathers ate in the land of Egypt. Whoever is hungry, let him come and eat. Whoever is needed, let him come and celebrate Passover. Now we are slaves; next year may we be free.

The middle matzah is broken in half. One half is put back between the two whole matzahs. It is a Moroccan custom to raise the Seder plate over the heads of all before the Maggid section while the Leader chants:

Bivhilu yatzanu mimitzrayim, halahma anya b'nei horin.

In haste, we went out of Egypt with our bread of affliction; now we are free people.

The other broken half is placed between napkins or cloth, designated the Afikomen (dessert), and put aside— often placed between the two pillows resting near the Leader.

5. The Story of Passover:

Maggid מַגִּיד

Why four questions? *(Hmmm. Guess that makes it five questions.)* We're here to celebrate freedom from slavery. As a slave, one is not entitled to free will or the ability to question authority or even have an opinion. We are now free to ask, to question, to understand, and to be heard.

The youngest gather and ask collectively or individually in Hebrew, then English. The same adult responds:

Ma nishtanah ha-lailah ha-zeh mi-kol ha-leilot?

מַה נִּשְׁתַּנָּה הַלַּיְלָה הַזֶּה מִכָּל הַלֵּילוֹת?

Why is this night different from all other nights?

Same person responds to each question in English:

1. She'bechol halaylot ain anu matbilin afilu pa'am echat, halyla hazeh shtei pe'amim?

On all other nights we do not dip even once; on this night, why do we dip twice?

 The saltwater represents the tears we cried as Pharaoh's slaves. The maror in charoset symbolizes the sweetening of our burden of bitterness and suffering.

2. She'bechol halaylot anu ochlim chametz o matza, halyla hazeh kulo matza?

On all other nights we eat either bread or matzah; on this night, why only matzah?

 This commemorates the fact that our Jewish ancestors did not have time for their bread to rise when they hastily fled from Egypt. And, it serves to remind us that the Jews were poor and matzah is cheap and easy to produce.

3. She'bechol halaylot anu ochlim she'ar yerakot, halyla hazeh maror?

On all other nights we eat herbs or vegetables of any kind; on this night why bitter herbs?

 To remind us of how we shed tears due to the bitterness of slavery.

4. She'bechol halaylot anu ochlim bain yoshvin bain mesubin, halyla hazeh kulanu mesubin?

On all other nights we eat our meals in any manner; on this night why do we sit around the table in a reclining position?

 We commemorate our freedom by reclining on cushions like royalty of ancient times when they enjoyed meals.

 ALL: We were slaves to Pharaoh in Egypt and our Mighty Lord brought us out with a strong hand and an outstretched arm. We are commanded to tell the story of our Exodus from Egypt so we never forget that we—like many races and cultures—have endured the hardships of slavery.

The Maggid includes satisfying the needs of four different types of children: the wise, the wicked, the simple, and the son, who is unable to ask.

A young person asks each question and the same adult responds.

 What are the testimonials, statutes and laws our Lord commanded?

 You're wise to want to understand what is commanded of us. Tonight the laws unfold, starting with the creation of the Seder plate, to the partaking of the Afikomen, to reciting from Hallel. Patience and all will be revealed.

 What does this Passover service mean to you?

 This is not about me or you. This is about us. To remove yourself from our people or our history is disrespectful. Once you understand, you'll better appreciate the gift of freedom that we take for granted. We have all felt separate or removed, so what you're experiencing is normal.

 What is this Seder service?

 Ahh. You're like the "Wise" child—you too wish to understand. Friends and family are here tonight to help you understand. This is a story you'll never forget.

I don't know how or what to ask.

And there is nothing wrong with that. This is one of our Lord's 613 mitzvahs, or commandments: to "Tell your child on that day." All will soon make sense.

ALL: The Children of Israel groaned and cried because of their servitude; their cry rose up to our Lord. He heard their cries and sent Moses to have His people freed. Pharaoh's heart hardened and the result was pestilence.

We fill our cups and will remove one drop of wine as we recite each of the plagues to remind us of how our people and the Egyptians have suffered. Use a fingertip or tip of an eating utensil to place drops of wine on your plate. We recite each in Hebrew and English in unison:

1.   (Blood) — *Dam* דָּם
2.   (Frogs) — *Tze-phar-day-ah* צְפַרְדֵּעַ

3. (Vermin) — *Kee-nim* כִּנִּים
4. (Beasts) — *Arove* עָרוֹב
5. (Cattle disease) — *De-ve* דֶּבֶר
6. (Boils) — *She-cheen* שְׁחִין
7. (Hail) — *Ba-rahd* בָּרָד
8. (Locusts) — *Arah-beh* אַרְבֶּה
9. (Darkness) — *Cho-shech* חֹשֶׁךְ
10. (Slaying firstborn) — *Ma-kat Bechorot* מַכַּת בְּכוֹרוֹת

After the slaying of the firstborn, Pharaoh allowed the Jewish people to leave, but changed his mind and chased after them. Our Mighty Lord, with a strong hand and outstretched arm, miraculously caused the Red Sea to split, allowing the Israelites to cross safely. When the Egyptians entered the Sea, it returned to its natural state and unfortunately for our Egyptian oppressors, the Egyptian army drowned.

The Leader rises and holds up the Seder plate and points to each as someone else reads:

The Seder plate: Chazeret: bitter vegetables; Karpas: parsley; Maror: bitter herbs; Charoset: mixture of nuts and spices; Zeroah: shank bone (or whatever you wish to use to represent a shank bone); and Beitzah: roasted hard-boiled egg (or whatever you wish to use to represent a hard-boiled egg).

Discussion: The youngest had their opportunity to ask questions and I thank them for that. Their contributions are very much appreciated and our Seder wouldn't be complete without their help. Now it's my turn to ask a question or two. *(Please see "Discussion Topics," page 66.)*

We conclude the Maggid by singing an abbreviated version of Dayenu—acts G-d performed for the Israelites when they left Egypt. While still sober, our Leader will read the English while the rest of us sing the chorus:

If our Lord would have taken us out of Egypt and not executed judgment upon them, it would have been enough for us.

Da-da-ye-nu,
Da-da-ye-nu,
Da-da-ye-nu,
Da-ye-nu Da-ye-nu Da-ye-nu

If He would have executed judgment upon them and not upon their idols, it would have been enough for us.

Da-da-ye-nu,
Da-da-ye-nu,
Da-da-ye-nu,
Da-ye-nu Da-ye-nu Da-ye-nu

If He would have judged their idols, and not killed their firstborn, it would have been enough for us.

Da-da-ye-nu,
Da-da-ye-nu,
Da-da-ye-nu,
Da-ye-nu Da-ye-nu Da-ye-nu

If He would have split the sea for us, and not let us through it on dry land, it would have been enough for us.

Da-da-ye-nu,
Da-da-ye-nu,
Da-da-ye-nu,
Da-ye-nu Da-ye-nu Da-ye-nu

If He would have drowned our enemies and not provided for our needs in the desert for forty years, it would have been enough for us.

Da-da-ye-nu,
Da-da-ye-nu,
Da-da-ye-nu,
Da-ye-nu Da-ye-nu Da-ye-nu

Let us lift our wine cups and pray in Hebrew.

Baruch Atah Ado-nai Elo-heinu Melech Ha-olam Boreh Pree Ha-ga-fen.

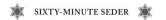
בָּרוּךְ אַתָּה אֲדוֹנָי אֱלֹהֵינוּ מֶלֶךְ הָעוֹלָם, בּוֹרֵא פְּרִי הַגֶּפֶן.

While reclining, we relish our second cup of wine.

6. Second Ritual Hand-Washing:

Rachtzah רָחְצָה

Those who wish may join in the washing of the hands. Please remove any rings and note this time the prayer is recited. And if our dear, dear host has not forgotten—the prayer will be written on a note near the sink. While still wet, both hands are lifted as the blessing is recited.

When the Leader exits to the kitchen is the best time for the youngest to "steal" the Afikomen and quickly hide it.

Baruch Atah Ado-nai Elo-heinu Melech Ha-olam Asher Kid'shanu B'mitzvotav V'tzivanu Al Nitilat Yadayim.

בָּרוּךְ אַתָּה אֲדוֹנָי אֱלֹהֵינוּ מֶלֶךְ הָעוֹלָם, אֲשֶׁר קִדְּשָׁנוּ בְּמִצְוֹתָיו וְצִוָּנוּ עַל נְטִילַת יָדָיִם

Blessed are You, Lord our God, King of the Universe, Who has sanctified us with His laws and commanded us to wash our hands.

After washing one's hands, it's important to refrain from speaking until reciting both blessings for the matzah.

A guest who hasn't washed their hands rises and recites the following:

Pesach—This is a Passover offering for our Lord, Who passed over the houses of the Children of Israel in Egypt when he struck the Egyptians and spared our houses.

He/She now holds up maror:

Maror—The Egyptians embittered the lives of our fathers and mothers with hard labor, with mortar and bricks. It's our duty to praise, honor and bless Him, Who performed the miracles that led to our salvation.

The Leader holds up the three matzahs for all to see until all eat:

Matzah—They baked the dough they brought out of Egypt into unleavened bread since it had not fermented and couldn't rise.

7. Blessing Before the Seder Meal:

Motzi מוֹצִיא

Please recite two blessings in Hebrew:

Baruch Atah Ado-nai Elo-heinu Melech Ha-olam Hamotzi Lechem Min Ha-aretz.

בָּרוּךְ אַתָּה אֲדוֹנָי אֱלֹהֵינוּ מֶלֶךְ הָעוֹלָם, הַמּוֹצִיא לֶחֶם מִן הָאָרֶץ.

Blessed are You, Lord our God, King of the Universe, Who brings bread from the earth.

8. Blessing Over Matzah:

מַצה Matzah

Baruch Atah Ado-nai, Elo-heinu Melech Ha-olam, Asher Kid'shanu B'mitzvotav V'tzivanu Al Achilat matzah.

בָּרוּךְ אַתָּה אֲדוֹנָי אֱלֹהֵינוּ מֶלֶךְ הָעוֹלָם, אֲשֶׁר קִדְּשָׁנוּ בְּמִצְוֹתָיו וְצִוָּנוּ עַל אֲכִילַת מַצָּה

Blessed are You, Lord our God, King of the Universe, Who has sanctified us with His laws and commanded us to eat matzah.

The Leader now provides a piece of matzah from the top and middle matzahs for each to enjoy.

9. Eating the Bitter Herbs:

Maror מָרוֹר

Person next to the Leader rises and holds up the Maror:

You may eat your maror with or without matzah. Please recite with me in Hebrew only:

Baruch Atah Ado-nai, Elo-heinu Melech Ha-olam, Asher Kid'shanu B'mitzvotav V'tzivanu Al Achilat Maror.

בָּרוּךְ אַתָּה אֲדוֹנָי אֱלֹהֵינוּ מֶלֶךְ הָעוֹלָם, אֲשֶׁר קִדְּשָׁנוּ בְּמִצְוֹתָיו וְצִוָּנוּ עַל אֲכִילַת מָרוֹר

Blessed are You, Lord our God, King of the Universe, Who has sanctified us with His laws and commanded us to eat bitter herbs.

10. Matzah and Charoset Sandwich:

Korech (Sandwich) כּוֹרֵךְ

We make a sandwich using two pieces of matzah with maror and charoset (mixture of nuts, fruit, wine and spices) that symbolize the mortar used by the Jewish people to make bricks while enslaved in Egypt.

We now enjoy our incredibly unique sandwich.

11. Dinner:

Shulchan Orech שֻׁלְחָן עוֹרֵךְ

We remove the Seder plate and return it once the meal is finished. We start our meal with roasted egg dipped in saltwater. It not only reminds us of the tears of our ancestors but it takes the place of no longer slaughtering the paschal lamb, since the Jewish Temple no longer stands.

*Passover dinner is served and you're welcome to more wine.
Just no beer—unless you find some made kosher for Passover.*

12. The Afikomen (Dessert upon Meal Completion):

Tzafun צָפוּן

The Seder plate is returned to the table and whether an adult or child hid the matzah, it's brought back (after tough negotiations) so a piece of the Afikomen is eaten by each person present before proceeding.

13. Grace After the Meal:

Barech בָּרֵךְ

Third cup of wine is filled but we don't drink just yet.

Leader: Blessed is the Name of our Lord from this moment and forever.

ALL: Blessed is the Name of our Lord from this moment and forever.

Leader: With the permission of the distinguished people present, let us bless our God for we have eaten from what is His.

ALL: Blessed is He, our God, of Whose we have eaten and through Whose goodness we live.

Leader: Blessed is He, our God, of Whose we have eaten and through Whose goodness we live.

The following line is recited only if ten post–Bar or Bat Mitzvah are present:

Leader: Blessed is He and Blessed is His Name.

ALL: Blessed are You, our God, King of the universe, Who nourishes the entire world; in His goodness, with grace, with loving kindness and mercy.

בָּרוּךְ אַתָּה יְיָ אֱלֹהֵינוּ מֶלֶךְ הָעוֹלָם, הַזָּן אֶת הָעוֹלָם כֻּלּוֹ בְּטוּבוֹ בְּחֵן בְּחֶסֶד וּבְרַחֲמִים, הוּא נֹתֵן לֶחֶם לְכָל-בָּשָׂר כִּי לְעוֹלָם חַסְדּוֹ, וּבְטוּבוֹ הַגָּדוֹל תָּמִיד לֹא חָסַר לָנוּ וְאַל יֶחְסַר לָנוּ מָזוֹן לְעוֹלָם וָעֶד, בַּעֲבוּר שְׁמוֹ הַגָּדוֹל, כִּי הוּא אֵל זָן וּמְפַרְנֵס לַכֹּל, וּמֵטִיב לַכֹּל וּמֵכִין מָזוֹן לְכָל-בְּרִיּוֹתָיו אֲשֶׁר בָּרָא. בָּרוּךְ אַתָּה יְיָ הַזָּן אֶת הַכֹּל.

Ba-ruch a-tah A-do-nai, E-lo-hei-nu Me-lech Ha-o-lam,
Ha-zan et ha-o-lam ku-lo, b'tu-vo,
b'chein b'che-sed uv-ra-cha-mim,
hu no-tein le-chem l'chawl^ba-sar, ki l'o-lam chas-do.
Uv-tu-vo ha-ga-dol, ta-mid lo cha-sar la-nu,
v'al yech-sar la-nu, ma-zon l'o-lam va-ed.
Ba-a-vur sh'mo ha-ga-dol, ki hu Eil zan um-far-neis la-kol,
u-mei-tiv la-kol, u-mei-chin ma-zon
l'chawl^b'ri-yo-tav a-sher ba-ra.
Ba-ruch a-tah A-do-nai, ha-zan et ha-kol. (A-mein)

Sovereign God of the universe, we praise You; Your goodness sustains the world. You are the God of grace, love, and compassion; the Source of bread for all who live; for Your love is everlasting. In Your great goodness we need never lack for food; You provide food enough for all. We praise You, O God, Source of food for all who live.

ALL: The Compassionate One, may He make us worthy of the days of the Messiah and the life of the world to come. He Who makes peace in His heavenly heights, may He make harmony for us and for all Israel. Let us say, Amen!

We pray that He who establishes peace in the heavens grant peace for us, all Israel, and all of humankind, and let us say, Amen as we rise, take hands and sing for peace.

Oseh Shalom Bim-romav Hu Yaaseh Shalom Aleinu Ve-al Kol Yisrael Ve-Imru Amen

עוֹשֶׂה שָׁלוֹם בִּמְרוֹמָיו, הוּא יַעֲשֶׂה שָׁלוֹם עָלֵינוּ וְעַל כָּל יִשְׂרָאֵל. וְאִמְרוּ: "אָמֵן."

May the One who makes peace send peace to us and all of Israel.

Let us lift our cups of wine and pray in Hebrew:

Baruch Atah Ado-nai Elo-heinu Melech Ha-olam Boreh Pree Ha-ga-fen.

בָּרוּךְ אַתָּה אֲדוֹנָי אֱלֹהֵינוּ מֶלֶךְ הָעוֹלָם, בּוֹרֵא פְּרִי הַגָּפֶן.

We return to our seats and while reclining, take great pleasure in our third cup of wine.

Praise the Lord, all you nations; extol Him, all you peoples. For great is His love toward us, and the faithfulness of the Lord endures forever.

We welcome Elijah in our final five minutes of the Seder:

 Our final cup is filled while an additional cup is filled and set aside for the prophet Elijah (Eliyahu)—whom, it is firmly believed, will precede the arrival of the Meshiach.

 We all rise as the youngest will open a door to allow Elijah to enter as we chant Eliyahu Hanavi in Hebrew.

Eliyahu Hanavi, Eliyahu Hatishbi, Eliyahu Hagiladi, Bimheirah Yavo Eileinu Im Mashiach Ben David.

אֵלִיָּהוּ הַנָּבִיא אֵלִיָּהוּ הַתִּשְׁבִּי אֵלִיָּהוּ הַגִּלְעָדִי, בִּמְהֵרָה יָבוֹא אֵלֵינוּ עִם מָשִׁיחַ בֶּן דָּוִד

Elijah the Prophet
Elijah the Tishbite (Returning)
Elijah the Giladite (Mound of witness)
In haste and in our life may he soon come to us
With the Meshiach son of David. (x2)

ALL: Our God is in the heavens. He has done whatever He has pleased. Their idols are silver and gold, the work of men's hands. They have mouths but they cannot speak; eyes have they but they cannot see; they have ears, but they cannot hear; noses have they but they cannot smell; they have hands but they cannot feel; feet have they but they cannot walk; nor can they speak through their throat.

All are seated.

 They who make them are like them; so is everyone who trusts in them. O Yisrael, trust in the Lord: He is their help and their shield. O house of Aaron, trust in the Lord: He is their help and their shield. You who fear the Lord, trust in the Lord: He is their help and their shield. The Lord has been mindful of us: He will bless us; He will bless Yisrael.

 The dead cannot praise the Lord, nor can any who go down into silence. But we will bless the Lord from this time forth and forever more... Oh praise the Lord, all you nations: praise Him, all you peoples. For His love for us is great: and the truth of the Lord endures forever.

14. Praises and Blessings:

Hallel הַלֵּל

We close the door. If Elijah has arrived, we hand him his cup of wine and ask what to do next. If not we continue...

We believe steadfastly in the coming of the Messiah, though clearly we do not yet merit his arrival. We will wait each and every day for him. And now we will read portions of Psalms 113 to 118 as we prepare to conclude our Seder.

Psalm 113

We praise God for being so great, yet able and willing to save the lowliest human being: Praise the Lord! Praise, O servants of the Lord, praise the name of the Lord. Let the name of the Lord be praised, both now and forevermore. From the rising of the sun to the place where it sets, the name of the Lord is to be praised. The Lord is exalted over all the nations, His glory above the Heavens!

Psalm 114

We praise You Lord for being so great that You can deliver a nation that was enslaved to the most powerful nation on Earth, part a sea and a river, and miraculously provide water from a rock; and therefore You can meet all of our needs too!

Psalm 115

The Lord has been mindful of us; He will bless us; He will bless the house of Israel; He will bless the house of Aaron. He will bless those who fear the Lord, the small together with the great. May the Lord give you increase, you and your children. May you be blessed of the Lord, Maker of Heaven and Earth. The Heavens are the Heavens of the Lord; but the Earth He has given to the sons of men and women. The dead do not praise the Lord, nor do any who go down into silence; but as for us, we will bless the Lord from this time forth and forever. Hallelu-Yah! Praise the Lord!

Psalm 116

We praise God that He is able to save us from the most dire circumstances: I love the Lord because He hears my voice and my supplications. Because He has inclined His ear to me, therefore I shall call upon Him as long as I live. The cords of death encompassed me, and the terrors of Sheol (home of the dead) came upon me; I found distress and sorrow. Then I called upon the name of the Lord; "O Lord I beseech You, save my life!"

Psalm 117

ALL: We praise God that His salvation was designed to flow from Israel to the nations of the world: Praise the Lord, all you nations; extol Him, all you peoples! For great is His love toward us, and the faithfulness of the Lord endures forever. Hallelu-Yah! Praise the Lord!

Psalm 118

In my anguish I cried to the Lord, and He answered by setting me free. The Lord is with me; I will not be afraid. What can man do to me? The Lord is my helper. I will look in triumph on my enemies. It's better to take refuge in the Lord than to trust in man. I was pushed back and about to fall, but the Lord helped me. The Lord is my strength and my song; He has become my salvation.

Anah Adonai, ho-she-ah na! We implore You, O Lord, the true God who saves.

Let us pour our fourth cup of wine and pray in Hebrew:

Baruch Atah Ado-nai Elo-heinu Melech Ha-olam Boreh Pree Ha-ga-fen.

בָּרוּךְ אַתָּה אֲדוֹנָי אֱלֹהֵינוּ מֶלֶךְ הָעוֹלָם, בּוֹרֵא פְּרִי הַגָּפֶן.

While reclining, we consider how grateful we are to be together as we drink our fourth and final cup of wine.

15. Closing Section:

Nirtzah נִרְצָה

Baruch HaShem. We've finished the Passover Seder according to its precepts and customs and those who have stayed beyond the meal are to be commended.

Thank you for joining us for this year's Seder as we conclude, asking our Lord that if it be His will—the Meshiach will come to earth in our lifetime—when men and women of all nations will dwell in peace. And all misery, misfortune and turmoil will pass over each of us.

All together in English then Hebrew:

Next Year in Jerusalem

Lishana Ha-baah Bi-yerushalyim

לְשָׁנָה הַבָּאָה בִּירוּשָׁלָיִם הַבְּנוּיָה

Counting the Omer – *conclusion of the second Seder only:*

Ba-ruch A-tah Ado-nai E-lo-he-nu Me-lech Ha-olam Asher Kid-e-sha-nu Be-mitz-vo-tav Vetzi-va-nu Al Sefi-rat Ha-omer

Blessed are You, Lord our God, King of the Universe, Who makes us holy by Your Mitzvot and commands us to count the Omer.

(And conclude with reciting:)"Today is the first day of the Omer."

We encourage you to participate in a fun song or two. And it probably wouldn't hurt to enjoy a bit more wine.

To the Tune of "My Favorite Things" from The Sound of Music
Lyrics by Annette H. Landau

Cleaning and cooking and so many dishes
Out with the hametz, no pasta, no knishes
Fish that's gefilted, horseradish that stings
These are a few of our Passover things.

Matzah and karpas and chopped up charoset
Shank bones and kiddish and yiddish neuroses
Tante who kvetches and uncle who sings
These are a few of our Passover things.

Motzi and maror and trouble with Pharaohs
Famines and locusts and slaves with wheelbarrows
Matzah balls floating and eggshell that clings
These are a few of our Passover things.

When the plagues strike,
When the lice bite
When we're feeling sad
We simply remember our Passover things
And then we don't feel so bad.

To the Tune of "There's No Business Like Show Business"
by Rabbi Dan Liben

There's no Seder like our Seder,
There's no Seder we know.

Everything about it is Halachic
Nothing that the Torah won't allow.
Listen how we read the whole Haggadah
Sometimes in Hebrew
'Cause we know how.
There's no Seder like our Seder,
There's no Seder we know.

Moses took the people out into the heat
They baked the matzah while on their feet
Now isn't that a story
That just can't be beat?

There's no Seder we know
So now it's on with the show!

Go Down Moses ("Let My People Go")

When Israel was in Egypt's land,
Let my people go;
Oppressed so hard they could not stand,
Let my people go.

Go down, Moses,
Way down in Egypt's land;
Tell ol' Pharaoh,
Let my people go.

The Lord told Moses what to do,
Let my people go;

To lead the Hebrew children through,
Let my people go.

Go down, Moses,
Way down in Egypt's land;
Tell ol' Pharaoh,
Let my people go.

We need not always weep and mourn,
Let my people go;
And wear these slavery chains forlorn,
Let my people go.

Go down, Moses,
Way down in Egypt's land;
Tell ol' Pharaoh,
Let my people go.

Had Gadya – An Only Kid (Aramaic)
This is done at a brisk tempo. Okay to play a recording.

Had gadya, had gadya.
Had Gadya—One Little Goat
Had gadya, had gadya.

My father bought for Seder.
Had gadya, had gadya.
Then came the cat and ate the goat,
My father bought for Seder.
Had gadya, had gadya.

Then came the dog and bit the cat,
that ate the goat,
My father bought for Seder.
Had gadya, had gadya.

Then came the stick and beat the dog,
that bit the cat that ate the goat,
My father bought for Seder.
Had gadya, had gadya.

Then came the fire and burned the stick,
that beat the dog that bit the cat,
that ate the goat,
My father bought for Seder.
Had gadya, had gadya.

Then came the water and quenched the fire,
that burned the stick that beat the dog,
that bit the cat that ate the goat,
My father bought for Seder.
Had gadya, had gadya.

Then came the ox and drank the water,
that quenched the fire that burned the stick,
that beat the dog that bit the cat,
that ate the goat,
My father bought for Seder.
Had gadya, had gadya.

Then came the butcher and slew the ox,
that drank the water that quenched the fire,

that burned the stick that beat the dog,
that bit the cat that ate the goat,
My father bought for Seder.
Had gadya, had gadya.

Then came the angel of death,
and killed the butcher that slew the ox,
that drank the water that quenched the fire,
that burned the stick that beat the dog,
that bit the cat that ate the goat,
My father bought for Seder.
Had gadya, had gadya.

Then came the Holy One, blessed be He!
And destroyed the Angel of death,
that killed the butcher that slew the ox,
that drank the water that quenched the fire,
that burned the stick that beat the dog,
that bit the cat that ate the goat,
My father bought for Seder.
Had gadya, had gadya.

Glossary

Afikomen — "That which comes after" or dessert.

Ashkenazi — Jews of Central or Eastern European decent. More than 80% of Jews today are Ashkenazim.

Barech — Grace after meals.

Baruch HaShem — Blessed be G-d.

B.C.E. — Jews do not typically refer to the calendar using Christ to designate time, i.e., B.C. (Before Christ). Instead use B.C.E. (Before the Common Era) or C.E. (Common Era) instead of A.D. (Year of our Lord).

Beitzah — Hard-boiled roasted egg, symbolizing the festival sacrifice offered in the Temple in Jerusalem.

Berakhah — Blessing or prayer.

Bimah — Platform or reading table in a synagogue used when chanting or reading portions of the Torah and the Prophets.

Birkat Ha-Mazon — Grace after meals. Also referred to as bentshing.

Bitter Herbs — Red or white horseradish.

Chametz — Leavened products forbidden during Pesach.

Chametz Search — Final search takes place the night before Pesach. If Pesach falls on a Saturday night the search takes place Thursday night.

Charoset — In the Ashkenazi tradition, charoset consists of chopped apples, walnuts and cinnamon with a bit of red wine. The Sephardic tradition uses dried fruits such as figs, apricots and pears mixed with chopped walnuts and red wine. It represents the mortar the Israelites used to make bricks while they were slaves in Egypt.

Elijah — A 9th-century B.C.E. prophet who ascended to the spiritual worlds in a flaming chariot: The one chosen to announce the arrival of the Mashiach.

Haggadah — The traditional text of the Seder that is essentially what it was two millennia ago. The Haggadah is organized in two ways: Four cups of wine to demarcate four different moments in the Seder and the fifteen steps that intersect with the four cups of wine.

Halacha — (Halachic/Halachically)—Judaism is not based on what you believe but what you do and comprised of rules and practices. Halacha is Jewish Law or, literally, "The path that one walks."

Hallel — A chant of praise consisting of Psalms 113 through 118. Included but considerably abbreviated in this Haggadah.

HaShem — "The Name." Another way of saying "G-d."

Hecksher — A symbol certifying that something is kosher. Samples include:

When the product is kosher for Passover it will have a "P" next to the kosher symbol.
D-P is dairy kosher for Passover while M-P is meat kosher for Passover.

Kabbalah — Ancient Jewish mystical interpretation revealing how the universe and life work.

Kadesh — To sanctify or make holy. To rise above the mundane.

Karpas — Parsley, radish, celery, green vegetable or potato.

Kashrut — Jewish dietary laws.

Korech — To wrap or sandwich.

Kosher — (Kashrut) Satisfies the requirements of Jewish law.

Kosher for Passover — Meets Kashrut and Pesach rules.

Kvell — Beam with pride.

Maggid — "One who tells."

Maror — Red or white horseradish.

Mashiach — Messiah.

Matzah — Flat, unleavened bread made of flour and water. The dough must be removed from the oven before eighteen minutes have elapsed.

Mitzvah — Commandments. There are 613 in Judaism.

Mizrayim — Land of Egypt.

Motzi — "Who brings forth." Blessing for bread.

Nirtzah — "Acceptance." The Seder has been executed and completed properly.

Omer — A counting of each of the forty-nine days between the second night of Passover and Shavuot. Kabbalists view this as a time of reflection to prepare us for receiving the Torah.

Passover Time Line — The exodus occurred approximately 1400 B.C.E. and celebration starts the night of the 14th day of the first month (Nisan).

Pesach — "Passover."

Pharaoh — Ruler or king in Ancient Egypt. No certainty of who was Pharaoh during the time of the exodus.

Rachtzah — "Washing." Fascinating to find so many restaurants in Israel with sinks made available for the washing of hands prior to a meal.

Sabbath (Shabbat) — The Jewish day of rest starts sundown Friday and concludes sundown Saturday.

Seder — A Jewish ritual service and ceremonial dinner for the first night or first two nights of Passover.

Seder Plate — A plate containing the symbolic foods (except for matzah and saltwater) during the Passover Seder.

Sephardic — A Jew of Spanish, Portuguese or North African descent.

Shank Bone — Lamb or chicken leg bone.

Shank Bone for Vegetarians — Beet, turnip, or chunk of ginger.

Sheckeyanu — "Who has given us life."

Shiva — "Seven." After a funeral, mourners of a parent, sibling, spouse or child stay home until the morning of the seventh day.

Shul — Jewish Synagogue.

Shulchan Orech — A set table.

Todah Rabah — Thank you very much.

Torah or Tanakh — Five Books of Moses: Genesis, Exodus, Leviticus, Numbers and Deuteronomy.

Tzafun — Afikomen.

Urchatz — Wash hands.

Yachatz — "Divide." Breaking the middle matzah into two.

Yom Tov — "Holy Day." Standard greeting during holy days.

Z"l — Of blessed memory. May he/she rest in peace.

Second Night's Seder

We traditionally host the Seder the first night and if fortunate, are invited to another home for the second night. We're not permitted to prepare on the first day of Yom Tov for the second day. The only difference is that we start the *Counting of the Omer* on the second Seder. *Please see page 31.*

All preparation for the second Seder, including setting the table, is to start forty-five minutes after sunset. This includes lighting candles for the second day.

Kitchenware

This is where I give my wife unending credit and appreciation. Ideally you'll use completely separate eating and cooking utensils. Yes, that means what you use throughout the year is boarded up and stored until after Pesach. Separate pots, pans, dishes, silverware, coffee pots, cups, blenders, dish soap, dish towels, etc. (At least you won't need a separate toaster.) And, of course, if you're kosher, meat and milk will have their own kitchenware. So the kosher home will have four sets of dishes—two for Passover and two for the rest of the year. (It's costly to be an Orthodox Jew!)

We use glass dishes and cups since once cleaned, they can be used for meat or milk. We also use mostly paper plates during the week of Passover.

No food is to leave the kitchen on the day before Passover. Set aside a special space to stash the chametz you'll be selling for the duration of Passover. This can be a closet, kitchen cabinet, or a room in the basement, as long as it can be locked and made inaccessible during Pesach.

Those unable to make this Pesach kosher, please consider separate dishes (even on the cheap) or plastic or paper. Do what you can to make this experience as different as possible. You'll be surprised how much your guests will appreciate your efforts. And you may be pleasantly surprised at how rewarding it is to take that extra step.

Preparing the Seder Table

Like preparing the table for the bride of Shabbat, this is to be a truly special table—different from all other nights. Fine white linen (even though wine will surely be spilled), your best dishes and silverware, wine glasses (we use shot glasses since it is customary to drink four full glasses of wine), a small dish of saltwater at each setting, silverware, bowls with extra portions of each item found on the Seder plate and a wine glass set aside for Elijah. Also, stacks of matzah strategically located on the table(s).

Each guest will have his/her own copy of the Haggadah, and please include the children so they feel respected and part of the Seder. The three-matzah bag and the holder for the Afikomen are to be placed by the Leader. Place a chair next to the Leader with two pillows to leave the Afikomen.

It is our custom to have cushions on the seat of the Leader for reclining purposes. You may wish to provide one or two cushions for each guest. If you have children or elderly guests, it's a great idea to have some plates of vegetables/dip laid out so they can eat during the course of the Seder.

Yom Tov candles should be placed wherever works best. Just don't move them. Wine/grape juice bottles should all be opened before the Seder.

Some set a glass of water for Miriam next to Elijah's cup to honor her contributions to the Jewish people. For it was Miriam who foretold Moses's arrival with "My mother will give birth to a son who will redeem Israel..." and as a reminder of the life-saving "Miriam's well."

Some add an orange to the Seder plate honoring the GLBT community to show inclusiveness. Our Seders never distinguish between sexual orientations, but if this works for you, go for it!

And finally, place a hand towel and pitcher of tepid water near the sink along with a copy of the following prayer when washing the hands:

Baruch Atah Ado-nai Elo heinu Melech Ha olam Asher Kid'shanu B'mitzvotah V'tzivanu Al Nitilat Yadayim.

Eruv Tavshklin

This is a ritual regarding the cooking and food preparation on the second day of the holiday (Friday) for use on the Sabbath. To fully and adequately understand this process, we suggest you conduct an online search. Chabad.org is a reliable source.

Chametz

The Search:

The evening before Pesach, we use a candle (or flashlight) to conduct a thorough search for Chametz wherever it may have been brought in. Before the search, carefully wrap ten pieces of crumbs in paper and hide them throughout the house. Kids love to track them down. Just don't forget where you hid them. Besides the candle, it's customary to take along a feather and a wooden spoon. The crumbs will eventually be burned. Your search begins with the following Berakhah (prayer):

Bo-ruch A-toh Ado-noi E-lo-hei-nu Me-lech Ho-olom A-sher Ki-de-sha-nu Be-mitz-vo-sov Ve-tzi-vo-nu Al Bee-ur Cho-metz.

Blessed are You, our God, King of the Universe, Who has sanctified us with His commandments, and commanded us concerning the removal of Chametz.

After the search, gather all the Chametz in a bag in order to burn it the following morning. You'll probably want to set some Chametz aside for your evening's dinner or for breakfast the next morning. It's important to gather the final bits of Chametz and add it to what you found the night before for burning.

If Pesach begins Saturday night, the inspection is to take place Thursday night and Chametz is burned Friday before noon. Upon completion of the search, the following blessing is recited:

Kol-chamira va'chami'a d'ika virshuti d'la chamiteih ud'la chamiteih vi'arteih li'vtil ve'lehehey k'afra d'ar'a.

Any Chametz in my possession, which I did not see, and remove, not know about, shall be nullified and become ownerless, like the dust of the earth.

The Burning:

Burn the day of Pesach before noon. If Passover falls on a Saturday night, there is no burning. The leftover Chametz is to be flushed down the toilet before noon. After the flushing the following Berakhah is recited:

Kol-chamira va'chami'a d'ika virshuti da'chamiteih ud'la chamiteih d'vi'arteih ud'la viarteih li'vtil ve'lehevey k'afra d'ar'a.

47

Any Chametz in my possession, which I did not see, and remove, not know about, shall be nullified and become ownerless, like the dust of the earth.

The Keeping:

It's costly to get rid of all your Chametz, so there is a halachically correct way to keep everything—even that expensive jug of pure maple syrup you bought just a few weeks ago. Work directly with a Rabbi for this simple process or fill out a form on Chabad.org.

Or, work with a Gentile where you provide a bill of sale, giving him/her ownership of your Chametz. Set it aside so it's inaccessible. You can store it during Pesach since it's not your property. The bill of sale should indicate you're selling the Chametz at a specific price and if the buyer fails to pay you by the time Passover is over, you regain possession.

Invitations:

Depending on your guests' level of understanding/experience, you may wish to give them a sense of what to expect and recommended attire. There are no set rules for what to wear in our home. Just keep in mind that you want this night to be as special as possible so it really is "different." Some may ask specific guests to prepare to lead a short discussion on a specific topic.

Candle Lighting Assistance:

Candles are lit eighteen to twenty minutes before sunset. If on a Friday night, light Pesach candles before lighting Shabbat candles. Some light two candles while others light one candle per family member. Our custom, having three children, is to light five candles for Shabbat and two for holy days. Once candles are lit, they are not to be moved (or as a Gentile overnight guest once did, thinking she was doing us a favor) blown out before going to bed for the night.

The woman of the house covers her head with a scarf, lights the candles, stretches her hands toward the candles, moves them inward in a circular motion three times, covers her eyes with her hands and recites the prayer. It's common to recite a personal prayer. This is such a beautiful means to bring light into the lives of all attending your Seder.

Please see page 1 for the candle lighting prayers.

Children's Activities:

Bottom line: Kids need to create or assist so they're given a sense of pride and ownership. Instead of "My *parents'* Seder," it becomes "*Our* Seder."

If they're going to create crafts, they'll want to start well in advance. There are numerous craft books and websites to help explain how these crafts can be made inexpensively. This is simply food for thought:

- Create an Afikomen holder.
- Create a bag for the three matzahs, with a divider so all are separated.
- Design and create Seder plates. Paper or plastic works.
- Create a Kiddush (wine) cup for Elijah.
- Decorate placecards if you prefer to designate where guests are to be seated.
- Decorate individual placemats.
- Create pillow cases decorated or covered with matzah-looking material.
- Create a chametz feather.
- Make their own coloring books. Download black and white images to color.
- Create or decorate a child's bib.
- Decorate an apron for each person creating the meal.
- Create individual name tags if your guests don't know each other.
- Help prepare the Seder meal.
- Ask them to rehearse *The Four Questions*.
- Encourage them to set up the Seder plate(s).

The more involved the young ones are, the more they'll look forward to and participate in the festivities. And remind the Leader to acknowledge their contributions at the start of the Seder.

Seder Plate:

It's our custom to provide a plate for every four to six guests.

Maror: Horseradish — whole or grated. Not a problem to use the red or white that is commercially made. Must be KP. If not, please make sure it doesn't contain corn syrup.

Chazeres: Romaine lettuce will also serve as a bitter herb.

Charoset: Grated apples or other fruits, nuts, cinnamon and other spices mixed with red wine. Eventually mixed with Maror during the Seder.

Z'roa: Roasted bone with some meat on it. (Can certainly be celery stalk, parsnip or bone made of clay instead.)

Beitzah: Roasted hard-boiled egg—a symbol of mourning. (Beet or avocado seed for vegans.) It's a Jewish custom to eat hard-boiled eggs with the first meal after a funeral. The egg is a symbol of life and hope for those sitting Shiva. During the Seder, we dip the egg in saltwater to remind us that our life at times, as with our ancestors, brings tears.

Karpas: Celery, parsley or boiled potato.

Matzah: Do not put on the Seder plate. Three matzahs are placed on top of each other and separated by napkin or cloth. We typically add a basket of matzah covered with napkins, in reach of maybe six guests. It makes it a lot easier when they can help themselves during the Seder.

Saltwater: Not put on the Seder plate. Prepare beforehand. Our custom is to provide a small dish at each setting. Wouldn't it make you feel special to have your own serving of saltwater?

Simple Matzah Meals for the Week of Passover

Matzah Brei

Break up your matzah in four or five pieces. You don't want the pieces to be very small. Hold the matzah under the water for just for a second. Don't soak it. Crack a couple of eggs into a large mixing bowl and add your matzah, but don't soak it; just soften it so it absorbs the beaten eggs. Then go ahead and fry. It typically cooks very quickly. Sprinkle with sugar and cinnamon or add veggies, salami, or both for variety. This is an all-time favorite.

Coffee Matzah

Break up matzah in a cup of coffee. Some enjoy adding milk and sugar.

Pizza Matzah

Cover matzah with tomato sauce and grated cheese and place in a toaster oven. You might want to add a bit of oregano and some black olives. I would send at least a dozen with my son Ian when he was a teenager for his school lunches. His Gentile friends *insisted* he share his "Jewish pizza."

Matzah Tuna Sandwich

Make your favorite tuna salad or add finely chopped onions, celery, dill, parsley, mustard, mayonnaise plus additional seasonings and sandwich in between a couple pieces of matzah. Try topping it off with some avocado or sprinkle some cheese on it and turn it into a delicious tuna cheese melt.

Matzah, Cream Cheese and Jelly

Please make sure your jelly is free of corn syrup. *It's only eight days.*

Matzah in Matzo Ball Soup

Cass also likes to add lettuce. (I know: He's strange!)

Meal Suggestions for the Seder

I can't stress enough about using fresh fruits and vegetables during Passover. After all, they are already kosher for Passover. It will keep your grocery bills lower and keep the waistline from growing. The prepackaged products for Passover are costly and have little or no food value for the calorie content. It is a great time to experiment with some raw food recipes or even some recipes for juicing.

As Cass already mentioned, the main thing about observing Passover and having a Seder is to make it different from the rest of the year. Eliminating leavened products and all grains is one way. Using different dishes is another. And certainly, gathering family and friends for a Seder service is the most special way of all.

So here's our menu. Most of these recipes can prepared with some help from the children. They like to be included, too.

Hard-Boiled Eggs

Hard-boil enough eggs so each guest has one and there are extras for the Seder plates. I always make extra because some get damaged during peeling. Purchase eggs at least a week ahead so they aren't too fresh. Fresh eggs are harder to peel. Place the eggs in a pan, cover with water, and bring to a rapid boil. Place a lid on the pan, turn off the heat and allow to sit for 30 minutes. Then drain and cover with ice water.

Charoset

The primary ingredients are apples, nuts and wine, and then you add things to your own taste. I use Fuji apples, walnuts, chopped dates, cinnamon, honey and wine. Chop the apples and walnuts to a fine consistency. When mixed together it should hold together to represent "mortar." This can be made the day before or the morning of the Seder.

Maror

Cass likes small pieces of the whole horseradish root. I guess it's the "manly" thing to do. I love fresh grated horseradish with beets. It takes some work, and I recommend making it a few days ahead. Have the tissues ready because you are going to cry!

Fresh Horseradish and Beet Puree

- 2 cups peeled horseradish root (12 ounces before peeling)
- 1/2 cup raw beets, peeled and finely chopped (or drained canned beets)

- 3/4 cup apple cider vinegar or distilled white vinegar
- 1/3 cup sugar
- 1/2 teaspoon kosher or coarse salt

Shred the horseradish. You can use a food processor with a shredder blade if you have one, but a sturdy cheese grater or box grater will work in a pinch. Transfer horseradish to medium bowl. If you are using a food processor, switch to the metal blade and return horseradish to work bowl. (If you don't have a food processor, a blender works well for the next step.) Add beets, vinegar, and sugar. Process until almost smooth, scraping down sides of bowl to ensure even mixing. Add the salt. Place horseradish in glass jar with a tight-fitting lid and chill overnight before serving. It can be stored in the refrigerator for up to ten days. Remember, you can always buy the already-made stuff but this is really tasty. Beware: Many bottled horseradish sauces have corn syrup. Who knew?

Now for Your Splendid Seder Meal

Matzo Ball Soup

In all humility, everyone loves my Matzo Ball Soup. I'm sharing my "secret" recipe for this Haggadah. That alone is worth the price of the book.

Start with the Manischewitz box of Matzo Ball and Soup mix. It's vegetarian, easy and just needs a few things added. For a group of six or more, use two boxes. Follow the package instructions for making the matzo balls. Be sure to refrigerate the dough for the 20 minutes as instructed. You need a large soup pot with a tight-fitting lid. Fill the pot with the correct amount of water as indicated on the box. Add the seasoning packet(s). For each box of mix, add one pound of peeled baby carrots that have been chopped or cut into thin rounds. Also add a half of a head of chopped cabbage for each box of mix.

Bring all of this to a boil. Once the matzo ball dough has chilled for 20 minutes and the soup is boiling, it's time to drop the matzo balls. Using a teaspoon, make walnut-sized balls and drop into the gently boiling broth.

Once they're added to the broth, cover the pot and lower the temperature to low/medium. Cover with the lid and DO NOT remove the lid for the entire 20 minutes of cooking time. This ensures the matzo balls will be light and fluffy. The soup can be made early in the day and reheated for dinner.

NOTE: Kids love to help make the matzo balls. Ask them to roll them into small balls and when they're done, you can drop them into the broth. Get them into the broth and covered with as little time lapsing as possible.

Aunt Ethel's Chicken Casserole
From *That Hungarian's in My Kitchen*
(Five Star Publications, Inc.)
One of my favorite recipes (serves 6).

- 2 tablespoons vegetable oil
- 1 cup chopped onion
- 1 cup chopped celery
- ½ cup chopped green pepper
- 1 chicken (fryer) cut up
- 2 tablespoons Worcestershire sauce
- Sea salt and pepper to taste
- Paprika to taste
- Garlic powder to taste
- 1 cup ketchup
- 1 cup water
- 2 tablespoons brown sugar

Sauté vegetables in the vegetable oil. Put chicken in casserole and brown in oven for 10 minutes. Add Worcestershire sauce and spices to the chicken. Cover the chicken with vegetables. Using a two-cup measuring cup, combine ketchup, water and brown sugar. Mix thoroughly and pour on top of the chicken.

Cover with foil and bake at 350 degrees for 1½ hours.

Vegetarian/Vegan Alternative

Use this instead of the meat dish or in addition to it. Quinoa is a seed and a great replacement for rice during Passover. It has superb nutritional value; it is a complete protein, a good source of nutrient-dense antioxidants, and is a great source of fiber and complex carbohydrates.

Quinoa-Stuffed Peppers
Serves 4 as a main course or 8 as a side dish

- 2 cups quinoa (pronounced "keen-wah")
- 2 cups water
- 4 red or yellow bell peppers
- 1 cup chopped walnuts
- ½ cup golden raisins
- 2 teaspoons olive oil
- 2 cloves minced garlic
- 3 tablespoons fresh parsley (chopped)
- 3 tablespoons chopped fresh mint (optional)
- 2 cups tomatoes (chopped)
- 6 green onions (thinly sliced)
- Sea salt & pepper to taste

Bring the quinoa and water to a boil in a saucepan over high heat. Reduce heat to medium-low, cover, and simmer until the quinoa is tender; about 15 to 20 minutes.

Preheat oven to 350 degrees. Lightly grease a small baking dish. Halve the red peppers lengthwise. Remove the seeds and ribs, but leave the stem intact so the pepper bowls hold their shape; place cut-side-up into the prepared baking dish.

Toss the olive oil, garlic, parsley, mint, tomatoes, and green onions. Fold in the quinoa and season to taste with salt and pepper. Fill the cut peppers with this mixture and fill the baking dish with about 1/4 inch of water.

Bake in preheated oven until the peppers are tender and the quinoa is hot; about 20 minutes.

Roasted Asparagus
Kids love to do the snapping – serves 6

- 2 bunches of thin asparagus - tough ends snapped off.
- 3 tablespoons olive oil
- Kosher salt
- 2 tablespoons minced shallot (or red onion)
- 2 tablespoons balsamic vinegar
- Freshly ground black pepper

Preheat the oven to 450 degrees. Spread the asparagus on a rimmed sheet pan and drizzle with the olive oil. Season with salt. Roast about 20 minutes, tossing halfway through, until the asparagus are tender and crisp at the tips. Sprinkle the asparagus with the shallot and balsamic, season with black pepper, and toss well. Roast for 2 more minutes.

Arrange the asparagus on a platter and drizzle with the liquid left in the sheet pan. Serve warm or at room temperature.

Paprika Potatoes
Cass's favorite—serves 8 to 10

Okay, this is a tough one to figure out amounts so prepare yourself to work with me. These are great reheated, so make plenty for leftovers.

Four pounds peeled potatoes—cut into small cubes, cover with water and a teaspoon of kosher salt and boil until tender. Once the potatoes are tender, drain thoroughly and allow them to sit in the pan to "dry" a bit.

While the potatoes are cooking, chop three very large sweet onions into small pieces. This should total about 3 to 4 heaping cups of onion. Sauté in olive or canola oil. The onion should be covered with the oil and cooked until clear and tender. Once the onions are cooked, turn off the heat, and add 2 tablespoons of sweet Hungarian paprika. Mix well and pour over the potatoes. If the potatoes seem dry, you may add additional oil or I like to use non-dairy margarine. (This is because we're having chicken and don't mix dairy and meat.) If you aren't serving meat, you can use real butter.

Cover the potatoes in the pan to keep warm and transfer to a serving dish when it's time to enjoy.

Israeli Salad
My favorite

This salad requires a lot of advanced chopping and can be made the day before. As far as amounts, it's really up to you. The main ingredients are the cucumber and tomato, so make enough for about ½ cup for each person. Chop all of the following ingredients into *small* pieces:

- Cucumber (seeded)
- Tomatoes (seeded)
- Radishes
- Sour or dill pickles
- Red onion
- Fresh parsley

Dress with olive oil and lemon juice to taste. You may also use salt and pepper. This is really delicious. We learned to love it when visiting Israel.

Nellie's Glazed Matzah

Spread a whole matzah with softened butter or margarine. Sprinkle with cinnamon and sugar and sprinkle on a few chocolate chips if you like. Place under the broiler or in a toaster oven until topping bubbles. This can also go in the microwave for 1 minute.

You can break this into small pieces as a dessert and serve with fresh fruit, or you can serve them for breakfast.

Easy Flourless Chocolate Cake

This is a dense and very rich "cake." Serve it with ice cream, whipped cream, or just a dusting of powdered sugar and fresh fruit. Raspberries are perfect. It doesn't get any easier than five ingredients and only three steps to follow.

I use raw cacao powder. This way, you're getting healthful benefits, including antioxidants, iron and magnesium in this decadent dessert. Another secret is to use a quality springform pan with a tight seal so you can peel the ring from the cake without marring it.

- 8 large eggs
- 1 cup raw cacao powder
- 1/2 cup butter, melted and cooled slightly
- 1 1/4 cups granulated sugar
- 1 teaspoon vanilla

Preheat your oven to 325 degrees.

Beat the eggs for 3 minutes at medium speed, until they're bubbly and light in color.

Measure the cacao powder by spooning into a cup. Do not compress. Add the sugar to the cacao and mix. Add by the spoonful to the eggs while mixing. While the mixer is running, drizzle in the melted butter. Continue beating until mixed. Scrape the batter into the pan.

Bake for 30 to 40 minutes. Cool on a wire rack and then place in the refrigerator to chill. The cake will become dense as it cools. Dust with powdered sugar if you desire.

One final suggestion: After eating all of this great food, you might want to "lighten up" for a few days. We recently discovered juicing and use it as meal replacements several times a week. Here is our favorite:

- 6 kale leaves (without stems)
- 1 cucumber (peeled if it isn't organic)
- 4 celery stalks
- 2 apples
- ½ lemon (peeled)
- 1 thumb-sized piece of fresh ginger (peeled)

This makes two very nice 12 oz. servings and it is very refreshing!

Discussion Topics

Permit fifteen minutes for discussion. Consider assigning someone a section of the Haggadah to study before they arrive. People might bring readings or questions based on what they're assigned, a poem or a reading that relates to the Seder, or simply use one of the following suggestions.

Please keep in mind there are no correct answers. These are opinions. Select one and have back-ups in case few are comfortable responding:

1. Share a short story of your experience of an exodus or finding freedom or justice. It could be the departure from a job, a career, a community, or maybe good health. There's much in life we leave behind, by choice or otherwise.

2. Yachatz, breaking the matzah, symbolizes the broken-ness of the Jewish people. Name one thing in our world that's broken and how to fix it.

3. We invite those who are hungry and needy to the Seder. What are some causes of poverty, and what is one thing we can do to help alleviate poverty?

4. In spite of freedom from Pharaoh, are we enslaved to vices, habits, behaviors or practices and if so, how do we break free?

5. Christians and Jews have a great deal in common when it comes to celebrating Passover and Easter. I'd like you to respond to (one at a time, please) what is their relationship to the following: Spring...Eggs...Shank Bone...Actual Seder Event...Bread & Wine...Death & Rebirth... New Beginnings...Miracles...Hiding & Seeking.

6. Why did G-d employ the drawn-out process of ten plagues in order to convince Pharaoh to free the Jewish people? Couldn't He get the same results by starting with the tenth plague? He is, after all, All Knowing, so He would know the first nine wouldn't work. (Responses should be interesting.)

7. Think back to when someone asked you a question (or you asked a question of yourself) that had a powerful impact on you. How did the question impact you and why?

8. Moses is clearly one of the most heroic individuals in the history of Judaism. Who do you know personally who is a hero and why?

9. Why do you think Moses is only mentioned once in the Haggadah?

10. Fleeing a country for freedom is not a new experience for Jews. Would a few of you share an experience where you or a member of your family fled one country for the safety of another? (Maybe advise them prior to the Seder that you'd appreciate their input.)

If your guests clamor for more time in discussion, suggest that once the Seder is over "We will sit around *(with yet another glass of wine)* and continue." This is usually both rewarding and exhilarating. *(Just don't talk politics!)*

Fast of the Firstborn *(or Not)*

This is touchy since there's a vast difference between Halachically and being politically correct. If a woman's child is a male child and born of natural birth, the firstborn male child must observe a fast the day of Passover—commemorating being saved from the plague of the firstborn.

Some believe *every* firstborn, male and female, whether of the mother or of the father, must fast. If there are no children, then the oldest member of the house is obligated to fast. If in poor health, it isn't necessary to fast.

Or Not. Some eat small portions before Passover begins so they don't enter the festival suffering. I was often able to avoid the fast by calling in late for work on the morning of the Seder and attending a brief Torah study at our Synagogue. A small meal is typically served after the service, making it permissible to eat the rest of the day. Bottom line: do what you can.

Epilogue

Since 2002, I have worked with Christians who desire to have a better understanding of their Jewish roots.

That desire is fueled by the fact that more and more Christians are coming to realize and understand that Jesus was a Jew and lived as a Jew and that He celebrated and participated in the traditional Jewish feast days and holy days and observed Jewish traditions.

The fact that Jesus Himself observed the Passover drives Christians to learn more about their Jewish heritage.

Over the years I have come to realize that many Christians are not very patient and will not sit through and participate in a liturgy that takes several hours.

That is why I am excited about the *Sixty-Minute Seder,* because in a short period of time, it exposes Christians to the joys and richness of the Passover liturgy and helps teach about the Jewish roots of Christianity so we can better understand our standing with G-d and the direction He has for our lives.

The lessons contained in the *Sixty-Minute Seder* are many: G-d's delivering power from bondage, His provision in times of need, His discipline in times of rebellion and His promise of hope and glory.

It is thrilling to see new and exciting approaches to the traditional Seder meal especially as it relates to the liturgy of the seder meal.

I believe the *Sixty-Minute Seder* will touch all age groups who participate in the Passover Seder meal.

- Rev. Jerry Clark, M.Div. currently serves as Director of Church Education for the International Fellowship of Christians and Jews. He has organized and led groups to Israel since 1997 and actively travels the country serving as primary teacher for Passover Seder meals.

About the Authors

Cass Foster, Professor Emeritus of Theatre, continues to be actively involved in the theatre as an educator, director and playwright. In the early 1990s, he wrote a series of *Sixty-Minute Shakespeare* plays so the standing joke at his long, drawn-out Passover Seders was "How about a *Sixty-Minute Seder* this year? Please!" And he admits, "Over the years I've put many a Seder guest to sleep and as I got older, I found I was even putting myself to sleep. So I figured an hour-long version might not be a bad idea." Then it occurred to Cass that others might appreciate a condensed version of the Seder as well. And not only Jews: "We have numerous Gentile friends and relatives who attend Seders. I suspected they'd appreciate a service lasting less then two to five hours that provides everything they need to know and everything they need to do."

Nellie Foster has spent her entire adult life in the medical field, from managing and creating medical labs to working as an educator in the field of infertility to serving as the Director of Clinical Operations in a naturopathic college in Tempe, Arizona. Nellie's experience in preparing Seder meals every year for as many as fifty guests has resulted in her delicious recipe contributions for both the Seder meal and the week of Passover. When not directing her energies in Passover-

related realms, she keeps busy as an actor, a board member for a couple theatrical companies and with her natural allergy relief practice www.CallNellie.com.

Email Cass & Nellie about your experience with the *Sixty-Minute Seder: Preserving the Essence of the Passover Haggadah* at SixtyMinuteSeder@gmail.com.

- Photo by Timory McDonald, Aloha Ever After

About the Contributors

Judith HaLevy has served as Rabbi of the Malibu Jewish Center and Synagogue since 1996. She holds advanced degrees in International Relations from both Rutgers University and Columbia University, and spent her early years in International Education in Mexico City and Tel Aviv.

Rabbi HaLevy has been a member of the executive committee of the Los Angeles Board of Rabbis since 2002 and was installed as president of the Board of Rabbis of Los Angeles in May 2011. She is a senior fellow at the Shalom Hartman Institute in Jerusalem, having completed three years of intensive study in the Rabbinic Leadership program in 2010. She is known throughout the Los Angeles area as a gifted teacher and speaker.

Jack Moline has served as Rabbi of the Agudas Achim Congregation in Alexandria, Virginia since 1987. He was ordained in 1982 by the Jewish Theological Seminary in New York, attending campuses in Los Angeles and Jerusalem. He graduated from Northwestern University and served as Director of Youth Activities for Seaboard Region of United Synagogue and interim director of the Hillel Foundation at the University of Virginia.

Rabbi Moline is currently chair of the board of The Interfaith Alliance, a national advocacy organization, and vice-president of the regional Rabbinical Assembly. Rabbi Moline is the author of *Growing Up Jewish*, a book of humor, and *Jewish Leadership and Heroism*, a sourcebook published by United Synagogue Youth.

Rev. Jerry Clark M.Div. was ordained into the ministry in 1994 with Calvary Ministries, Inc., International in Fort Wayne, Indiana. He entered the ministry in 1987, serving as an associate pastor of Calvary Temple Worship Center from August 1990 to May 2001.

Rev. Clark received his B.A. and Master of Divinity degrees from Christian Bible College and Seminary in Independence, Missouri. He currently serves as Director Church Relations for the *International Fellowship of Christians and Jews*, having joined the organization in January 2002. Rev. Clark has traveled to Israel numerous times since 1997 and has led and organized Christian tour groups to Israel from across America.

About Six Points Press

A Division of Five Star Publications, Inc.

Linda F. Radke, President

An industry leader in creativity, innovation and customer service since 1985, Five Star Publications, Inc., sets the bar for partnership publishing and professionally fulfilling traditional publishing contracts. An award-winning company, Five Star is committed to helping authors of all ages continually reach new heights.

Six Points Press specializes in publishing books that celebrate the rich Judaic culture. These books are either of Jewish interest or written by a Jewish author. Six Points Press offers books for readers of all ages and interests. The genres represented in Five Star Publications' growing collection include educational titles, nonfiction, picture books, cookbooks, juvenile fiction, memoirs, Westerns, novels, professional "how-to's" and more.

Along with providing book production and marketing services, Five Star Publications president Linda F. Radke and her team also assist organizations with website redesign, logo design and corporate/product branding. The work of Five Star contributors is also showcased

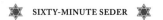
among leading corporations, nonprofit organizations and print, radio and broadcast media venues nationwide.

Five Star believes in contributing a portion of proceeds from book sales to various charitable organizations. It is a small way of making a difference, one book at a time.

www.SixPointsPress.com

Order Form

ITEM	QTY	UNIT PRICE	TOTAL
Sixty-Minute Seder: Preserving the Essence of the Passover Haggadah by Cass (Yickezkale) Foster & Nellie (Nechama) Foster (ISBN: 978-1-58985-260-0)		$12.95 US $13.95 CAN	
SHOAH: Journey from the Ashes by Cantor Leo Fettman (ISBN: 978-1-58985-258-7)		$14.95 US $15.95 CAN	
That Hungarian's in My Kitchen! 125 Hungarian/American/Kosher Recipes by Linda Foster Radke (ISBN: 978-1-877749-28-5)		$14.95 US $15.95 CAN	
Mr. Monday and Other Tales of Jewish Amsterdam by Meyer Sluyser (ISBN: 978-1-58985-007-1)		$14.95 US $15.95 CAN	
Sixty-Minute Shakespeare Series: Adapted by Cass Foster			
A Midsummer Night's Dream (ISBN: 978-1-87774-937-7)		$8.99 US/CAN	
Hamlet (ISBN: 978-1-87774-940-7)		$8.99 US/CAN	
Macbeth (ISBN: 978-1-87774-941-4)		$8.99 US/CAN	
Much Ado About Nothing (ISBN: 978-1-87774-942-1)		$8.99 US/CAN	
Romeo & Juliet (ISBN: 978-1-87774-938-4)		$8.99 US/CAN	
Taming of the Shrew (ISBN: 978-1-58985-220-4)		$8.99 US/CAN	
Twelfth Night (ISBN: 978-1-87774-939-1)		$8.99 US/CAN	
		Subtotal	
* 8.8% sales tax – on all orders originating in Arizona. **Tax**			
* $8.00 or 10% of the total order – whichever is greater. Ground shipping. Allow 1 to 2 weeks for delivery. **Shipping**			
Mail form to: Five Star Publications, Inc. PO Box 6698, Chandler, AZ 85246-6698 **TOTAL**			

NAME:

ADDRESS:

CITY, STATE, ZIP:

DAYTIME PHONE NUMBER: FAX:

EMAIL:

Method of Payment:
❏ VISA ❏ MasterCard ❏ Discover Card ❏ American Express

Five Star Publications, Inc.
P.O. Box 6698 • Chandler, AZ 85246-6698
(480) 940-8182 • (866) 471-0777
Fax: (480) 940-8787
info@FiveStarPublications.com
www.FiveStarPublications.com

**For information on how to
order an eBook go to:**

❏ Yes, please send me a Five Star Publications, Inc. catalog.
How were you referred to Five Star Publications?
❏ Friend ❏ Internet ❏ Book Show ❏ Other

78